THE JOURNEY OUT

How Are You Handling God's Plan?

THE JOURNEY OUT

How Are You Handling God's Plan?

Deborah E. Ransey

Publisher
JohnsonTrax Productions & Publishing, LLC
Houston, MS

Copyright 2024 by Deborah Ransey

All rights reserved. No portion of this book may be reproduced, stored in a retrieval system, or transmitted in any form or by any means: electronic, mechanical, photocopy, recording, scanning, or other—except for brief quotations in critical reviews or articles, without the written permission of the publisher.

To request permission, contact the publisher at Johnsonsprogress@gmail.com

First Printing: 2024

Paperback: ISBN 979-8-218-37387-0

JohnsonTrax Productions & Publishing, LLC
Houston, MS 38851
www.unfinishedclay.org

Note: All scripture references are taken from the Holy Bible KJV

Dedicated With Love

This book is dedicated to my Lord and Savior, Jesus Christ! Without Him I am nothing.

To my family, Kelvin Ransey, Sr., the love of my life, my best friend, and spiritual covering! You sir are amazing, and I can't imagine my life without you in it. Thank you for choosing me and giving me a wonderful family and church family! SOE and UIC you rock!

To my firstborn, Kierra Renee' Ransey. You are forever in my heart! There is not a day that goes by that I don't miss hearing your voice, seeing that special smile, our heated debates, and most importantly feeling your arms hugging me. I had to include you in this journey as you also made me a better person.

To my one and only son, Kelvin Ransey, II, I honor the man you have become while remembering the young son who loves me wholeheartedly! Your daily greeting when I returned home from work made life a little sweeter especially when my day was a total wreck! I proudly take another role in your life as I watch you flourish in your marriage with your beautiful bride Katelyn! I love the two of you and can't wait to see all that God has in store for you both. I am enjoying seeing you two grow in Jesus and in love. Stay committed to each other and God! You have made me proud!

To Marjorie and Keyra! I am one proud Auntie! You both have surpassed anything I could have imagined, and I am forever grateful for your unwavering love and belief in our family and me. Marj, there is so much I could say, but I will simply pen a big THANK YOU for everything. Thank you for the dinners, being a housekeeper even though it didn't pay lol, being a babysitter, and most of all being the prayer warrior and fighter in our corner! I love ya kid!

To my friends and family, my book club partners, and my dear family far and near, thank you all for loving me!

Lastly, to Lady Shae Reel-Johnson. You have stretched me by your belief in my gifts! You pushed me for this, and I am eternally grateful! You have supported me in my plays, my preaching, insecurities, and in my writings. I truly thank God that He placed you in my life! I can hardly wait to see what all that God will do in your life!

I pray that to whomever reads this book that you will be blessed and know that it is written only by the Grace of God. To God be the Glory.

Table of Contents

Introduction: Giving God the Pen –Kierra Ransey. p11

Shattering Cycles p21

Stuck in the Wilderness p25

The Fear of Moving Forward...................................p31

Follow His Instructions...p39

Identifying Your Fuel..p45

Give Up! Surrender!...p53

Transformational Promotion....................................p63

Conclusion: Are You Ready to Go?........................p73

About The Author...p75

GIVING GOD THE PEN

I'm a pretty good writer. Or at least I think I am. Writing comes easy to me effortlessly. While it may take other people two or three drafts to get a piece right, I can produce something really good in one sitting. I'm creative. I am the type of writer who learns the rules so I can break them.

While I am only a pretty good writer, I am a much better reader. Ever since I learned to read, I have been fascinated by the world of books. I was probably the only little girl who spent her summers in the library, but I loved it.

I'm not writing this to be an insufferable braggart. I'm trying to make a point. I know stories. I know what good stories are made of. I know how they are supposed to begin, progress, and end. I can spot a good story from a horrible one. Most of the times, I can predict a whole book or a movie in the first few minutes.

I'm a pretty good writer. I am an excellent reader. I know stories.

So, imagine my surprise when I go to pray this morning. I had some things on my mind, and I felt the urge to pray about it. I walked to my bedroom with the words already on the tip of my tongue. Those words never came out because as soon as I got quiet, God started speaking to me. He said a simple four words, but those words pretty much blew my mind.

Give me the pen.

I think I would have had a better time accepting this request if I were not an English major in undergrad. It's not like I can't write a good story. It's not like I couldn't tell a simile from a metaphor or understand what Deus Ex Machina means in terms of plot development. I AM A WRITER! I am a reader. I know stories. I've spent the last 7 years studying and creating them. I felt like God could trust me with the pen. I felt like I could trust myself with the pen.

You're a good writer Kierra, but I am a great writer. You're creative, but I am the Creator!

God has this funny and annoying habit of shutting me up. I don't really know why I continue to argue with God. Then again, this is the person who had the nerve to argue about who is more creative with the one who thought the Niagara Falls into existence. You don't even have to shake your head because I am shaking my head at myself.

I started thinking about the stories that God writes and they are more masterful than Shakespeare's works. I mean, think about Joseph's life. His story is nothing short of a work of art. God gave him a dream. He shared that dream with his brothers who wanted to kill him. They didn't kill him, but they threw him into a pit and sold him to the Egyptians. He ended up serving Potiphar only to be thrown in jail for doing the *right* thing. He helped someone while he was in jail and the person who he helped forgot about him for two years. Finally, one day, Joseph is summoned before the king. He helps the king and is suddenly given a position with power, authority, and riches. That's not the end of the story. He eventually became reunited with his brothers, saved their lives, forgave them, and preserved the bloodline of his family.

Joseph's story is a beautifully tragic story. I'm sure Joseph never envisioned being trapped in a pit when he had that dream. I can also go out on a limb and say that if Joseph were to write his own story, there would be no pit or prison in it at all. He wouldn't have had to go through anything. He wouldn't have had to cry. The thing is Joseph's story isn't beautiful despite the pit, it is beautiful *because* of the pit. The struggle was not only necessary, but it was beautiful. It was artwork. If Joseph would have edited out the hard times, he would have edited out some of the most moving parts. I bet the story that Joseph would have written for himself would have been good, but the story that God wrote for Joseph was much better: pit and all.

It's easy to read one of God's stories, but it is MUCH harder to be a character in one of them. Especially if you are a control freak like I am. It's hard to be a character because characters don't give input into their stories. Characters are the creations. They don't have to do, they just exist. The problem with us (okay, the problem with ME) is that we have a hard time of giving God the pen. We think we know what is best for our lives. We don't want to go through any hard times, but we desire "Happily Ever After" immediately. We can write stories that we could be comfortable with, but those stories pale into comparison with the story that God wants to write for us.

Give God the pen. Relinquish control of your life. Surrender. Trust the process. The stories that God writes aren't really the ones we want to be a part of, but at the end of the story, we will look back and see that the entire story was perfect: pit, prison, tears, and all.

From the heart of, Kierra Renae March 4, 2014.

The blog above was written by my beautiful daughter Kierra. She transitioned home to live with Jesus on August 16, 2018. It still seems like a dream some days that she is no longer here with us on Earth, but it is true. Nevertheless, she left so much of herself here in the Earth with us through her writings. What was once a pastime hobby and outlet of verbal expressions have now become precious, timeless pieces of her mind process and her conversations with her Father God that we have grown to cherish and learn from. Kierra taught me a valuable lesson through this specific writing. The lesson is that, even though we hold life's pen in our hands, our story is already prewritten by the Master Author, God. We can only write (live out) what He has ALREADY WRITTEN! Every detail of our life's journey has already been mapped out with a master plan in mind. Every mishap, misturn, mistake, misunderstanding, and mismanagement of our time has been accounted for by Him. Yet, it did not alter the plan.

For me, traveling around in circles has been an insane challenge and experience! Why would anyone choose to continue the cycle of repeated failures and dismal results when aiming for a promised future and victory? In the pages of this book, my hope is that you find a clear path to enlightenment and future victory in your own life. The journey out can be challenging but rewarding! When you begin to break unhealthy habits and cycles, you can expect positive changes to life's circumstances, discovery of unhealthy boundaries, and revelations concerning relationships and demonic placements of people who have been planted to hinder your progress. Does what you see align with what He said concerning you? This is my coming out story! I will not proclaim that I've mastered this faith walk, but I will say that I'm walking! I am learning to trust God's plan over mine. It is an exciting journey, and it began with shattering cycles! Let's walk together!

Notes

Chapter 1

SHATTERING CYCLES

"You can't break what you are unwilling to acknowledge."

The first thing that one must do is acknowledge behaviors that cause repeated patterns. I have heard it said that insanity is doing a thing systematically the same every time while expecting a different outcome. This is one thing that hinders many people as they travel along life's road. Sometimes people continue walking in a way that does not lead to their desired goals and outcomes, yet some kind of way they expect positive results over time. That is just not how that works. If you repeat the same patterns in life, you will always reap the same results of being hindered from reaching God's promises concerning your life. You must be willing to admit that what you are currently experiencing is a direct result of a continuous pattern you tend to repeat. Face the fact that what you are doing is not working for your betterment. Progress is a byproduct of troubleshooting and correcting faulty cycles. Negative cycles can be broken by refusing to hide behind excuses for repeated behaviors and facing issues head on.

Defective cycles can be classified as anything that pulls you away from the purpose and intent of your life's story. Adverse life events such as a failed career, divorce, family issues, financial burdens, or even failing health can form and trigger negative patterns which lead to defective fruit (results.) The Bible clearly states in 3rd John 1:2, "Beloved I wish above all things that thou mayest prosper and be in good health even as thy soul prospers." A defective cycle can eliminate this Godly desire from coming into fruition and manifesting in our lives. Our journey can be filled with repeated calculated limitations that bind our understanding, trust, and direction from God.

With all the above in mind, it is essential and beneficial for us to shatter defective cycles once and for all. In order to do this, discipline and temperance are necessary. They are both distinct characteristics of the fruit of the spirit! Galatians 5: 22-23 states, "But the fruit of the Spirit is love, joy, peace, longsuffering, gentleness, goodness, faith, meekness, temperance: against such there is no law." Shattering cycles can be challenging but doable by the help of the Holy Spirit. When you fail to shatter cycles, you may become stuck in a dreaded place called "The Wilderness."

Notes

Chapter 2

STUCK IN THE WILDERNESS

We must insert the characteristics of Christ into each of our situations to eliminate strong holds! Bishop Kelvin Ransey often states, "A strong hold is something that holds you strong." I like to think about it as a "wilderness experience." This is the place of stagnation and circles. It is the space where a person feels as if they are held hostage because there is somewhere they need to be, but cycles and patterns have clogged their engine of progress. It can be quite overwhelming knowing that you are destined and called to a place of promise, but every time you assess the situation you realize that you've only traveled in a big circle.

This can be EXHAUSTING! Let's move from this place! Let's travel together step by step. Let's do a few steps at a time. Here we go!

STEP 1: Acknowledge that you have existing negative cycles. You can't fix what you choose to ignore.

STEP 2: Identify triggers, patterns, and defective actions that hinder you from your specific goal. This step takes honest evaluation and accountability. I understand that there may be extenuating circumstances that complicate things even more, but what part do you play in the matter?

STEP 3: Be willing to let go of things and/or people who sit contrary to your next season of change. This is where you shed old habits, negative thoughts, and maybe even people who are

no longer called to walk with you to your blessed place.

These are all things that keep us stuck in our wilderness experiences. Let's use our Biblical family as a brief example. You know them well. I'm referring to the Children of Israel. We discuss them often, but we should really evaluate their situation from a human standpoint. These people were ENSLAVED for years. Because of this, they adapted to an "Egypt Mentality." They were literally programmed by harsh slave masters to repeat patterns daily. Could you imagine waking up daily to do the same things EVERY DAY regardless of how hard the tasks were? They cried out to God, but if we will be honest, sometimes we pray from muscle memory instead of a faith stance of expecting to be answered. Nevertheless, God did send deliverance by way of Moses, but they didn't foresee being dropped off in this middle ground of what we know to be the wilderness. Now they are thrust into trying to do "new things," and go to this "Promised Land," but the hinderance was not where they were physically. The journey was exactly what it was... an 11-day walk. How did 11 days turn into 40 years of circling the same mountain? May I suggest that the mountain that was defeating them was not physical but mental? Even though they were free physically, they were still bound mentally. That is what caused them to become stuck. We often discuss them as if we could never do that (go in circles), but we do it all the time. Sometimes it's little things that trip us up and cause us to tread over the same grounds. Be aware of the little foxes that destroy your vines.

The wilderness mentality can be shed! It's challenging but doable. Are you sick of being stuck in your wilderness? Who or what are you dragging along that needs to be cut, shed, or dethroned from taking priority in your life? You cannot allow yourself to be hindered by situations that you CAN control! Take a moment to read that again. YOU have control over these influences and or influencers! The Children of Israel had to learn to shed and bury the mentality of their past generation before they gained access to their promise. Some of your greatest battles don't come from outside situations, but they come from within your own family and community. They learned to cry while moving and hurting! Surely in 40 years they passed by tombs where their loved ones were buried but instead of mourning every single time, they found strength to keep it moving. They had to stop fussing, complaining, and fighting one another before they could bind together to fight the giants in the Promised Land. They had to gain new insight and get fresh revelation concerning God and how He NEVER left them, even though I am sure some days they felt deserted and all alone. The wilderness is tough, but it is still not an excuse in God's eyes. Did you hear me clearly?

Tough is not an excuse with God. It is just a place for us to pass through and not become stuck. I encourage you to acknowledge that you have hindering cycles, identify your faulty mindsets and patterns, and decide to let them go! Ask God for strength to help you take these three small steps to begin your journey! He has been waiting on you to make the first moves this whole time. I promise that what is ahead is much greater than the cycles and scenes you currently see!

Chapter 3

THE FEAR OF MOVING FORWARD

I refuse to tell you that it's an easy task moving forward. You must tell people 'No,' make calculated advancements, and make new decisions that lead to progress. Sometimes that's hard. Yielding to other people's wills is a learned behavior that must be broken. Prayer, fasting, and educating yourself on how to keep making positive gains can keep you from repeating cycles while taking possession of your promise.

One challenge you may face while moving in the right direction is establishing boundaries from outside influences that have no bearing on what God has instructed you to do or go! Outside influences have no power to alter the road in life God has ordained us to travel. Sadly, we lend them power whenever we fail to realize how unimportant and unnecessary they are to our lives. Outside influences must be left in the wilderness! If the people on the outside do not encourage you to take the Promised Land (exhibit a Joshua or Caleb mentality) but instead instill fear in you concerning moving forward in God (the 12 spies negative report), then they must be cut from your life! Period! I don't care if it's mother, father, sister, brother, cousin, or best friend! They must be left behind for you to reach your full potential. Oh, and let us not forget about the loud opinions of others as well that try to misdirect our steps from time to time. You must ignore opinions that are opposite to what God has proclaimed concerning you. These things and people are destiny blockers! Learn to cut off opinions that are contrary to what God has said to you. God's directions are precise. Granted, they may sound vague to your ears due to limited details, but His right now instructions to you are precise and important. Follow that voice. If He spoke to you today, then He will give you what you need for that set of instructions. Regardless of how good it sounds, NEVER allow anyone else's voice to amplify louder than God's. Never allow anyone to occupy God's space in your life. Be cautious of this (allowing man's voice to be louder than God) because frustration, failure, disappointment, and sometimes desperation will become your portion. Now I am not referring to confirming words of others because God will send messengers from time to time to confirm that you are still in line for your destiny. I am talking about the people that Satan sends to get you off course.

God is not an unstable God. He does not lead us haphazardly. He is not reactive nor proactive. He is ACTIVE! Every detail of your march forward is accounted for. So now, I will pose a few questions that I really want you to consider. The questions are, "What's hindering you from moving forward?" "Is it inward conflict or outward influence?" "Could it be a mixture of both?" In the above chapter, I gave a few steps that are vital to progress. Let's look again at step 3 to focus on it a little bit deeper. **STEP 3: Be willing to let go of things and/or people who sit contrary to your next season of change.** Before you can let go of things, you first must identify exactly what the problem is in the first place. Let's identify a few things that keep up from moving forward.

1. **Fear of trials, hardships, and demonic backlash.**
2. **Besetting sins and spiritual weights that weigh us down.**

Let's address number one: Fear of trials, hardships, and demonic backlash. You will always have battles to overcome. One tactic that Satan is notorious for pulling out of his bag of tricks is the spirit of fear: fear of the unknown, or fear of trying. He just wants us to be afraid, but if you focus on Jesus, the outcome of victory is inevitable. You will win EVERY TIME! Think about many of the battles that the Lord allowed His servants to engage in during biblical times. God gave them power to conquer when they consulted and acknowledged Him. When they followed God's instructions on how to engage in warfare they won! It was only when they relied on their own understanding that things went awry. Always consult God when facing decisions, issues, struggles, and challenges. His plan works for your good. Never fear demonic backlash. You have been granted power and authority over the enemy.

Secondly, let's talk about spiritual weights and besetting sins. You must shed the weight and the sin that keeps you bound to cycles. If you find yourself wrestling with the same issue every time progress is near, that's a good indication that you are tussling with a weight or besetting sin.

In Genesis, God gave man dominion over every fish in the sea, animals on land, and herb bearing plants for his nourishment. I'm sure you are asking where I am going with this thought process. Stay with me here. Some addictive behaviors are rooted in substances that God has already given us dominion and power over. Money is made from trees, liquor is made from fruits, cigarettes are made from plants, and food is a compilation of plants and animals (whatever you like to eat derived from either a plant or animal from land or sea.) We can abuse what was given to us as a good thing and can turn it into an addiction that causes us to spend what we don't have to gain temporary pleasures. Park here for a moment and ponder what is holding you hostage and what has no legal basis to become a hinderance or addiction in your life. What currently has power over you that originally you were designed to have power to resist?

Another big hinderance is sexuality. Sex was and is a beautiful union between man and woman. We mortals have mishandled and replaced what was originally intended as a natural depiction for spiritual union and oneness. Now many have strongholds in areas that were never supposed to exist! This temptation and bondage come with lust, and the enemy rides you hard to get you to succumb to unholy desires. Be of good courage my friend, for the Lord has already planned for your deliverance. Jesus and His work on the cross were sent to deliver us all from every chain and bondage.

Please know that you are a winner. You can conquer anything! With Jesus on your side, you can do all things! Do not fear moving forward any longer. Go and advance freely! Stop (take a second to consider who you are and who God has ordained you to be), stand (stand firm on that knowledge and in the power of God) and see the promise and take the land! The lessons you learned while being stagnant will not be wasted either. Nothing, NO-THING, can stand before you or your God. Since God is for you and has given you your marching orders, take up the spirit of Joshua and be strong! Be strong in the Lord and in the power of His might. Believe like Caleb and say that "I'm ready for my inheritance!" The time is now! MOVE!

Chapter 4

FOLLOW HIS INSTRUCTIONS

"Brethren, I count not myself to have apprehended: but this one thing I do, *forgetting those things which are behind*, and reaching forth unto those things which are before, *I press* toward the mark for the prize of the high calling of God in Christ Jesus" (Philippians 3:13-14 KJV). I love these scriptures. Paul is saying in a nutshell that, "I can't live in my past, for to do so would cripple my future! I must have tunnel vision to see only God's plan and not anyone else's!" That sounds amazing, doesn't it? Here is the onerous part though. Sometimes it's hard to know which directions to follow to obtain and reach the mark of the high call. Occasionally various voices try to serve as a roadmap to your spiritual success, and there are many directional signs placed along the way! Sometimes the signs are placed by Satan to serve as a detour to guide us off the path that God has laid before us, and sometimes we hang our own signs by choosing to go in directions contrary to God's will as well.

Follow the course set by God, the Author of your life. He wrote every detail of your story before He laid the foundation of the earth. Before God ever said, "Let there be," He mapped out a plan and created a destiny for you! Seriously! Can you imagine that the end of your story was written and sealed before anyone ever stepped into your book of life to begin reading and observing chapters and seasons? Your life choices were known to the King of Kings, and He FACTORED in every aspect of your life! He factored the time it would take for you to confront your fears and issues. He included the time it would take for you to embrace your future. He knew the day and the hour that you would cave in and whisper "not my will Lord, but I stand in agreement with Your Will! He knew and revealed a plan that was already in place so that you could finally take a leap of faith and cross over to your blessed Promised Land! Dear friends, FOLLOW HIM AT ALL COSTS!

Follow God's instructions even if the route seems foolish to take. Never compare other people's directions to your own because you may become distracted that it took them less time with seemingly better results. You don't know the truth of the journey of others. What they encountered was specifically designed for them. Comparison is a trick of Satan, and many who choose to look through those lenses end up depressed or even with suicidal thoughts! Never look over to use another person as your starting point or measuring stick of progression. Look to the One that made you. Our Heavenly Father never duplicated anything He ever made other than Himself in us! Everything He did and continues to do is original. Every tree He formed is different and unique. Birds are different colors and sizes, and every human has unique characteristics that set them apart from others. He never repeated miracles in the same manner. His mind is so vast that it would be hard for Him to repeat a way for your life to get victories. How could you think He wouldn't create a plan specifically for you and your situation that leads to your promise? He wants you to depend on Him and not someone else's 10 step plan or methods that may or may not work! He has a set plan that was designed specifically for you and intentionally with you in mind. How amazing is that concept! Please Follow His instructions! Let me give you another point that will help you tremendously when faithing this part of your journey! Are you ready to highlight this key point? Well, here it is **STEP 4**: **FOCUS!**

Do you remember me beginning this chapter with the words of Apostle Paul? No worries, I will give them to you again. "Brethren, I count not myself to have apprehended: but this one thing I do, *forgetting those things which are behind*, and reaching forth unto those things which are before, *I press* toward the mark for the prize of the high calling of God in Christ Jesus." (Philippians 3:13-14 KJV). Apostle Paul is letting us know that we must have a set focus! Our focus must be on present and future goals and not on past failures and mistakes. Now, take a minute to scan your inner thoughts, your heart, and your life's surroundings. What is currently contending for your focus? Have you completely lost focus on who you are and who

God is calling you to be? Are you finding it hard to get important things done but easy to procrastinate? Friends… regain your FOCUS! You'll never reach the mark without it!

Chapter 5

IDENTIFYING YOUR FUEL
Use what Happened!

Bear with me for a moment as I take a quick left in this chapter. In the previous four chapters we discussed the act of cycles and the negative effects they can have on our lives. Now, we really need to discuss the root of the issue. We need to uncover the pain of what happened in the first place. Did you know that most people's start of a cycle was the result of a traumatic event? So many beautiful souls (male and female) suffer in silence as they deal with depression, anxiety, and insecurities and they come off as repetitive, self-destructive behaviors. There is a measure of grace available to you to deal with this matter! You can use what happened to fuel your progress versus allowing it to continue to delay your destiny.

Each issue that has ever held you captive can convert into purpose for the development of what is necessary for your future. The issues blocked you intentionally and deliberately to keep you from understanding God's original purpose in some aspect of your life. Let's visit a few common roadblocks that can easily cause unwanted cycles and then shine a light on how they can possibly be used for fuel of progress.

> 1. **Sexual Perversion-** This category is so vast until it is almost impossible to discuss or pinpoint the cause behind the bondage. I will say this though: More people have dealt with the traumatic experience of being exposed to unsolicited sexual encounters than they care to admit. Whether they were molested,

raped, introduced to pornography, or whatever the case, such issues are hard to deal with sometimes. The memories and residue can be overwhelming. Mostly, the anger that can be associated with the spiraling cycle can be death gripping. Nevertheless, many people deal with this silently and have developed coping mechanisms just to function.

2. **Poverty**- this can be both physical and mental. Sometimes a person can be born into unfortunate circumstances. Sometimes a person can be doing well in life and a major traumatic turn can happen suddenly that they were unprepared for. This can lead to poverty. I describe those two incidents as a physical type of poverty. Neither person(s) in the above situation can help themselves. Furthermore, there are some people who may

house the spirit of poverty or what I call mental poverty. Spiritual poverty can be spotted by observing people who have health, talents, and opportunities to advance in life but choose not to do so. They do not capitalize on chances to progress financially nor mentally. You may find them spending all of what they gain sporadically and haphazardly which causes them to remain in a poor state. The parable of the Prodigal Son is a great depiction of spiritual poverty.

3. **Low Self Esteem**- It's important to understand that everyone who seems "happy and confident" is not exactly that. We live in a culture that is notorious for masking truth. People are good at hiding behind filters and visages. Smiles sometimes hide tears. Promiscuous images sometimes camouflage low self-worth. Not only this but also missed and

failed opportunities can cause low self-esteem as well. Let's not even mention the effects of rejection and loss and the residue they leave in our lives.

I cannot begin to even scratch the surface of what you may have negatively encountered in life that sent your life into a spiraling whirlwind of pain. Nevertheless, I feel the need to say again that there is indeed a measure of grace extended to you for your total healing. Why is it important for you to heal once and for all? I'm glad you asked. These experiences, which can be very painful to us, can translate into power for yourself and others. If the love of money has been a stronghold, know that the desire for wealth was intended for you to be in a place of debt free living or a place of prosperous existence! I did not say rich although some of you may have intended for riches. Money was never meant to hold you captive or be your sole desire to obtain. Relationships, especially the bad ones, can sometimes detour your progress as well. Many have been in relationships that caused major voids which led to chasing love in all the wrong places. On the contrary, sometimes the relationships caused a person to live behind a wall of distrust without the capacity to ever venture out again. Either way, the effects can be traumatic and stunt potential growth and progress.

I want to encourage you to use the weakness of your past traumas and issues and turn it into a positive experience that will cause you to become who God ordained and called you to be. You are fearfully and wonderfully made. Romans 8:28 would be a great reminder for you. "For we know that all things work together for good to them that love God, to them who are called according to His purpose." Those events did not feel good, nor in essence were good, but God promises to allow all events to somehow work together for our good. Get the help that you may need, find the purpose, and use it as fuel for your destiny.

Notes

Chapter 6

GIVE UP! SURRENDER!

Saying, Father, if thou be willing, remove this cup from me: nevertheless, not my will, but thine, be done. Luke 22:42 KJV

This chapter causes me to feel a certain type of way. Reason being is that God was telling me for years to surrender to Him. I thought I was living in total submission to Him, but to be honest I really wasn't. In the hidden corridors of my mind, I knew that more trust was required of me. I trusted God but not with my entire being. I had more to yield, and it wasn't that I wanted to be rebellious, but I was more afraid than anything. I was afraid of the unknown will of God for my life. Because I didn't fully know what God was trying to say to me, I went on a fast! During the fast, I heard Him! He answered me! Unfortunately, I began to share God's answer with a trusted source and due to my own insecurities, I allowed their voice to override what I heard my Father say. I allowed another voice to hinder me, and it became louder than the spirit of God that was trying to lead me. After that, I struggled even more with yielding to God's plan because the spirit of confusion had entered through the voice of others. I struggled for years shuffling through different trials and tribulations trying my best to gain the ground I had lost by not yielding to God totally. I never imagined that it would take me going through the worst hurt thus far of my life to yield to his perfect will.

  Walk with me back in time as I recall the day of August 16, 2018. The day began normal, and my husband and I were going about the daily routine of getting our morning started. Our daughter Kierra was home with us. She hadn't felt well earlier in the week, but it was nothing that she normally couldn't push past per usual. To make a long story short, she was talking with her dad, and she suddenly began having breathing trouble. I do recall her asking her dad, "Am I going to die?" He replied by telling her that she wasn't going to die and her statement behind that was, "I'm glad I am saved," as we awaited the ambulance. Our sweet Kee went home to be with the Lord a few hours later. I didn't see that coming. My husband didn't see that coming. Furthermore, we were completely devastated and unbelieving that this was God's plan! Surely, He could have come up with a different alternative! Seriously, there had to be a better way! Honestly, He could have even taken me! Most days I felt He should have! I didn't know just how much I would have to truly rely on and trust God just to deal with the grief and depression for the days ahead. Hard is an understatement. I was even mad at myself for a season because I felt that I could have prayed her back to life. Shock had completely overtaken me that day and I simply could not pray. I, the one who prays for EVERYONE and about EVERYTHING, could not pray that day! Now I know why... It wasn't God's will for me to pray. It was His will for me to trust Him.

Kierra Renee' Ransey! She was and is a phenomenal woman, writer, and thinker and she was committed to servanthood! She loves Jesus but was not accepted by many simply because of who her dad was. People wanted her spot and systematically tried to oust her from her place in life. She suffered low self-esteem and championed others she saw struggling with the same. She was truly loved by many, but she never fully realized just how loved and amazing she was here on Earth. Our daughter was tired; therefore, God took her home. My family and I weren't given an option of keeping her here with us. All the things that transpired that day was out of my control. I had one of two choices: 1. Drown in my sorrows and grief or 2. Accept and yield to the will and plan of God. Here is where I can honestly say that out of exhaustion, depleted emotions, and a broken heart, I surrendered! I submitted to HIS plans. By doing so I'm convinced that although His plan may not feel or look good to me, I can grow and walk through every valley of the shadow of death KNOWING that HE is with me! He was with me through the entire process (and He remains). He was there during my deep moaning and groanings while battling grief and depression, and He was present when I accepted His perfect will for my life. Not only do I accept His will, but I also AGREE with His will as well. That is a huge statement. I did not say that I will be happy with or feel good about every outcome, but I do trust His plan over anything I could ever come up with.

In hindsight, I now know that a person's good intentions are sometimes rebellion displayed as concern. What may have been instructed for their lives may not be the same advice for your journey. Therefore, learn quickly to only allow God's voice to direct you. Within yourself you already know God wants you to surrender your will to His. Jesus Himself surrendered to the will of His father. Listen, before the cross was the garden of Gethsemane, and in that place was the revealed plan of God. You must strengthen yourself in Him to be able to stand this next phase of your journey! What is your promise? What does it look like right now? I submit to you that it is more in depth than you could ever imagine or hope for! You have just scratched the surface, but the plan is vaster, and it will expand to reach a multitude simply because it is attached to bigger. It's attached to the will of God! Your story is not yours alone, but it is entwined with a body of believers and those that need you to speak into their spirit life eternal! So many need to know the love of the Father! They have been introduced to His laws and are familiar with the judgmental ones who act like the religious sect of Jesus's era. You know them. We call them the Pharisees and the Sadducees! In life these are represented by people who uncover your issues while covering their own problems. They heap coal on others while offering grace to a select few. I want to minister to the ones that man condemns! Paul would not have graced many of our pulpits! He was a sinner and a murderer! What good could come out of him? God had to fetch him because the church was too scared to step out of their comfort zone to reach him. The church has gotten comfortable with condemning what God has deemed redeemable! Our job is to get them to Jesus. Present Him righteously and watch Him draw the Peter's, Paul's, and Mary's of this day to Him.

As bad as it feels, some things require you to totally submit to the unknown plan of God without subscribing to your outdated habits and outside influences for validation. Sometimes God places you in solitude until you learn the lesson of, He is in control, and He has the answers. God will send you help when you get to the place of total submission to Him. Listen to Him whenever He speaks. Surely, He has a plan that involves places and people you need and must meet. Your prayers are necessary for them. Get over your need to be in control and surrender to the plan of God. It cannot be a partial surrender but a total and complete turnover to what He said. If what you are hoping and planning for does not line up with what God has in mind, let it go. Do not take your will into this new place. Allow God to adjust your thinking so that the outcome of this battle is different than the results of previously lost ones! See what HE sees. It's better than anything you can come up with. The design is to complete the vision. The big picture looks amazing! Some of us had to run and catch up while others were able to walk steadily towards the promise. My advice to you is just do it! Give up! Surrender!

Notes

Chapter 7

TRANSFORMATIONAL PROMOTION

This chapter is exciting because it represents the next phase of your life. It is beneficial to understand that God not only heals you from yourself, but He does it with purpose. All of what He does is part of an overall plan and a broader scheme than what we realize. The whole purpose of it all is for us to transform so that we can be promoted to the next phase of our lives. That alone should excite you. I know it does me!

When you are ready for next, you should expect a new anointing and mantle to accompany you for the next phase of your life. Elisha, the Old Testament Prophet, received a double portion of his anointing from Elijah his prophetic mentor. Joshua was the successor to Moses, and everyone after Jesus's resurrection can receive the Holy Spirit if all conditions are met. You are heading into a new place with more authority and leadership capabilities in the natural and in the spiritual realm! He never wanted you to remain in a position of brokenness but rather in a place of wholeness, victory, and abundance! Let's consider the Battle at Ai in the Bible during Joshua's day.

The story of Joshua's encounter with Ai begins in the Book of Joshua chapter 7. In the previous chapter Joshua and the Israelites fought the battle of Jericho, and with God's power they experienced a great victory. It feels great to win, doesn't it? Well, in verse 2 of the chapter, Joshua does something that we tend to do when we are comfortable after a great victory.

He considered others' points of view and their advice without FIRST going to God himself. The men that Joshua sent did not properly account for every aspect of the battle. They looked at Ai's size only. They never considered that although they were a small nation, they were determined to maintain and stand their ground. Ai came out and battled the children of Israel and defeated them with a mighty blow. Israel felt that just because Ai was small that they were weak also. That was not the case. Anything small can become mighty if you are fighting it without God. How many times have we allowed "small things" to linger, but those trivial things were major hindrances in our lives. Strategies that worked taking one domain will not be effective during this phase of the battle. You must have fresh instructions for new warfare. Let's delve deeper into what else caused the embarrassment and defeat for Joshua and Israel! Joshua chapter 7 verse 1 states: But the children of Israel committed a trespass in the accursed thing: for Achan, the son of Carmi, the son of Zabdi, the son of Zerah, of the tribe of Judah, took of the accursed thing: and the anger of the Lord was kindled against the children of Israel (KJV). There was hidden sin! Let's stop for a second and think about that! A WHOLE NATION lost a battle due to a person connected to them having HIDDEN SIN! It wasn't even supposed to be known, yet GOD KNEW! Sin must be dealt with! Furthermore, the sin was one of disobedience. God did not allow disobedience to prosper and win, and He is the same now. Connections matter! Get rid of the offender and the offense because the sin will make you look like a fool! You must do everything according to God's directions to win even the smallest battles in your life!

When I think of Ai in the Bible, I can't help thinking of Ai in today's time. Today we call Ai "Artificial Intelligence." It is on our phones, tv's, home and car devices that allows us to communicate with any computers in our vicinity! It can create any illusion imaginable. It can even think and make decisions for you. This thing tracks your moves and gives out information to keep you tied up into bondage. If you want to lose weight it shows you good foods and creates you a whole meal plan, but it does not chase nor eradicate the root cause of the negative behavior to begin with. We can't be distracted by technology and tools that create easier paths but deny us total freedom. Consult God on every detail because it is **HIS** instructions that you will need to win life's battles spiritually and physically!

Promotion Ready

In verses 6-10 of Joshua chapter 7, Joshua was embarrassed, hurt, and defeated. He literally thew a spiritual tantrum. He was so ashamed that such a little army defeated him and his Army ESPECIALLY since they named the name of the God of Abraham, Isaac, and Jacob. Here is the good thing I see in the scripture. In verse 10, God speaks and gives directions. God explains thoroughly why they lost the battle and how to correct the problems to be successful and victorious once again. That's a good place to praise God right there! Sometimes we mess up horribly through our own disobedience. Nevertheless, when we go back to God and repent, He never withholds information that causes us to win! He created us to win! Winning is our portion in every aspect of our lives! He looks to promote us. Yet, we must do like He instructed Joshua! We must confront and eliminate the accursed things that God frowns upon in our lives, even when the things seem valuable to us. What good is it to hold on to something that is valuable but cursed? Obedience is better than sacrifice.

When Joshua obeyed God, he was promoted to win once again. The scripture declares in Joshua 8: 1 "And the Lord said unto Joshua, Fear not, neither be thou dismayed: take all the people of war with thee, and arise, go up to Ai: see, I have given into thy hand the king of Ai, and his people, and his city, and his land" (KJV). When we do what God says according to His instructions, we win! EVERYTIME! When you obey God, you are then qualified for promotion. Here is where the rubber meets the road, **TRANSFORMATION.**

In the transformation stage you must "Let this mind be in you which was also in Christ Jesus." (Philippians 2:5 KJV). He must be immersed into you, and you immersed in Him. When you are that intertwined in Christ, your concentration and focus will be on what is important to God the Father. To transform, you must be in Christ and Christ must be in you! Old mindsets must be left behind and allow the mindset of Christ to change the old you. We walk by faith and not by sight. You may still feel or see residue of the old person you were, but that is not who you are. You are **THE WORD** that God spoke over you and concerning you. Now elevate your mind to think like Him. When Christ went through the most difficult situation of His calling (His garden of Gethsemane) His response was, "Not my will but Thy will be done." That was transformation in action. He was at His humanly weakest, yet He transformed to the will of His Father. Christ went through Hell so that you can walk in victory. That's why the scripture says, *"These things I have spoken unto you, that in me ye might have peace.*

In the world ye shall have tribulation: but be of good cheer; I have overcome the world (John 16:33 KJV)."

Take that mindset with you into every aspect of your life and watch God cause you to transform and triumph. You can have what you ask of Him according to His will. You can think higher than the old ways you used to operate in, and you can walk in freedom, wealth, wholeness, and soundness of mind without the guilt of sin chasing you. You have been washed in the blood of the lamb and baby you are now His child! You belong in His royal family! You are covered by Him so come out of the old and into the new in Christ. It is His will for us to prosper! It is His will for us to dominate! It is His will that no matter what life brings, you can face it and still bless His name. Transformation is exciting and necessary! Wait no longer! Transform for promotion today!

Notes

Chapter 8

ARE YOU READY TO GO?

I want to encourage you to move forward! The time is now, and you are needed for a time such as this. I want you to know I am personally rooting for you as you journey into the next phase of your life in Christ. Function like the saint you are! Fight from the point of victory! Remove things that are keeping or holding you hostage and take back the vision and victory in His power and might!

You are not merely one in a million. You are strategically positioned to conquer and lead others in how to navigate this life we live. People are depending on your obedience to the Lord's divine orders concerning you! Stand firm and trust God to lead you through your wilderness. Just do whatever He says. Your triumph is linked to God's voice. It will work! You may need to separate yourself from specific people to get the victory. Lay aside everything that has caused you to stumble and fail. You are a winner ONLY when you battle with the Lord at your side! Finish this thing so your next season of conquering and possessing the land will flow without delay! Lastly, you must decide whose and who you are. You have a cloud of witnesses that can testify that if you stay focused God will lead you all the way! You have mountains to climb, visions to see, dreams to acquire, and fresh territory to conquer!

Get up and decide that today is the day to move forward and never look back. Thank God for your **JOURNEY OUT!**

Author Bio

Deborah 'Debbie' Elaine Ransey, a shining example of grace and dedication, was born in Toledo Ohio. She is the 5th child of 8 and graduated from Macomber-Whitney Highschool in 1977 and later obtained her Bachelor of Social Work from the University of Mississippi in 2017. She is the devoted wife of Bishop Kelvin Ransey and loving mother of Kierra and Kelvin Ransey II and bonus daughter Marjorie Patton. With unwavering faith and an unshakeable belief in the potential for positive change, Deborah serves alongside her husband as Co-Pastor and Elder of Spirit of Excellence Church in Oxford, MS. Despite their demanding roles, she still finds time to pursue her passions - baking, reading, and playwriting. A true beacon of light, Deborah's optimism and integrity inspire all of those around her. Her love for family and worship are paramount in her life, and she approaches each day with enthusiasm and anticipation.